TO THE GREAT SPIRIT

First Impression 1941
This edition 2020

© SPIRITUAL TRUTH FOUNDATION 2020

This book is copyrighted under the Berne Convention. No portion may be reproduced by any process without the copyright holder's written permission, except for the purposes of reviewing or criticism, as permitted under the Copyright, Designs and Patents Act 1988.

ISBN 978-1-9998571-9-6

www.spiritualtruthfoundation.org

TO THE GREAT SPIRIT

A Selection of Prayers

by

Silver Birch

The Spiritual Truth Press

INTRODUCTION

THIS booklet has been published in response to widespread requests from people who have asked that a selection of the prayers offered by Silver Birch, spirit guide of Hannen Swaffer's home circle, should be available.

At the beginning of every seance, Silver Birch has given an invocation to "The Great White Spirit." This has been his invariable practice during the whole of the nine years that his weekly trance utterances have been recorded.

From these prayers you will gain an insight into the spirit view of the Infinite Intelligence which is behind the universe. Silver Birch's conception of Deity is vastly different from that presented by Orthodoxy. He does not envisage a personal God made in man's likeness, with human limitations and passions. He does not restrict the manifestation of a divine architect to one church, one volume, one sect, or one being.

He constantly pays tribute to the natural law, which he says is immutable, never fails, and is directed by perfect love and justice.

Silver Birch is not concerned with theological dogma, ritual or doctrine. His appeal is always to reason. He believes that prayer should be an incentive to service, and worship a spur to labour.

To him the Great White Spirit is to be found in the operation of His natural laws and in the deeds of altruism and sacrifice performed by His children, in each of whom there resides a portion of His divinity.

Silver Birch's outlook is epitomized in his own dictum: "Our allegiance is not to a Creed, not to a Book, not to a Church, but to the Great Spirit of Life and to His eternal natural laws."

OH, Great White Spirit, we turn to Thee to seek guidance from the fountain of Thy infinite wisdom, to draw strength and sustenance so that we may be enabled to reflect Thy love, Thy teaching, to those who need it most.

Oh, Great Spirit, Thou art the perfect law, fashioned by the perfect mind. Thou, Whose spirit broods throughout all the universe, Who art manifest in every facet of natural life, has set Thyself within all human beings, so that for ever Thy spirit is linked with theirs by the tie of divinity. They can never remove themselves from Thee; they can never be separated from Thee; they cannot be where Thou art not.

Our mission is to teach mankind how to order its life that the innate divinity may rise to the surface and obtain a full expression. Then will there be dissipated all the jealousy and greed, all the selfishness and envy, all the hatred and malice, all those shortcomings which belong to the remnants of man's animal ancestry. The attributes of Thee will become exhibited, Thy compassion, Thy mercy, Thy loving kindness, Thy sympathy, all those forces which represent goodness at its highest and best.

To those who have lost their way, to those whose eyes are filled with tears, to those who wander in the darkness, to those who are hungry and thirsty, to those who are tired, weary and perplexed, we strive to bring them within the radius of spirit power, so that it may touch them and enable them more clearly to understand life's purpose and to see their place in Thy infinite scheme of creation.

Our whole labour is directed towards serving humanity so that it may understand itself and Thee and all the laws which control life in its varied manifestations.

OH, Great White Spirit, Thou art the law, the wisdom, the love, the knowledge and the inspiration.

We praise Thee because Thou art the centre of all life, for with Thee there is life and without Thee there is nought, for Thou dost pervade all life and Thy laws sustain and embrace all. We know that Thou hast placed within all human life a portion of Thy spirit, which brings all peoples together in unity with Thee.

We do not pray to Thee on bended knee, cringing with fear, ashamed of our inheritance, but we pray to Thee with knowledge and in the light of all that we have received, knowing that we are part of Thee and Thou art part of us. We stand before Thee, children of Thee, knowing that Thy spirit is within us, always seeking to rise higher in expression and to fulfil Thy law through us all.

We thank Thee, oh Great Spirit, for the opportunity to manifest to the children of earth the greater laws of the spiritual realms, so that, with their co-operation, we may be able to serve Thee and the world of matter by revealing Thy wondrous plan, so that the knowledge of Thy laws will enable all peoples to understand the purpose for which Thou hast placed them in the world of matter, so that Thy knowledge shall banish all ignorance, Thy strength shall drive away all weakness, Thy light shall illumine all the darkness and all suffering and misery shall be replaced by joy and by happiness.

OH, Great White Spirit, teach us what Thou art, and show us how to understand Thee. Throughout all time Thy children have tried to explain Thee, but Thou art greater than their explanations.

They have tried to capture Thee in churches, in temples, in mosques, but Thou art greater than all the constructions of earth. They have sought to limit Thy spirit in the pages fashioned by Thy children, but Thou art greater than all Thy children have conceived.

Because of Thy spirit, everything in the universe lives. Because of Thy spirit, the sun shines, bringing life and light into the world of matter. Because of Thy spirit, the rain drops from Thy heavens, bringing refreshment to all the growth that is necessary to Thy children.

Because of Thy spirit, all the manifestations of Nature raise their paean of praise to Thee, the Great White Spirit of all. Because of Thy spirit, all Thy children, whether encased in matter or whether freed from its limitations, turn to Thee, asking that they may understand Thee and act in unison with Thee.

Great Spirit, fill us all with the desire to serve wherever we can, so that each one of us can reflect Thy spirit wherever we go, and to all those who seek Thee. May we be uplifted so that we may reflect Thee always.

OH, Great White Spirit, how shall we express Thy infinitude? How shall we explain Thy laws, Thy wisdom, Thy knowledge, Thy love? How shall we explain the great infinite spirit of all, Whose breath gives life throughout all the universe and Whose eternal laws control every phase of living?

Oh, Great White Spirit, Thou Who art beyond the heights of imagination, Thou Who cannot be described in earthly language, Thou Who art mightier than the mightiest, lovelier than the loveliest, wiser than the wisest, Thou Who art king of kings, the creator and sustainer of all life, how shall we express Thee to those who do not understand Thee?

We do not look for Thee within the limitations of material things. We know that Thy majesty cannot be circumscribed within the limits of books. We know that Thou art beyond the restrictions of churches and beyond even the visions of prophets. And so we seek to reveal Thee in the operation of those eternal, natural, immutable, unchanging laws, realizing that Thy spirit permeates all places, all life, all motion, all rhythm, all pulsation and all harmony, and Thou art expressed within every manifestation of being, from the highest to the lowest, from the greatest to the smallest, from the majestic to the infinitesimal.

We would teach Thy children to find Thee within themselves, to hear Thy message as it is conveyed by the nodding of flowers, the swaying of a leaf, the drone of the insect, the beauty of nature. We would teach Thy children to find Thee in the infinite expressions of nature's changing beauties, so that they may learn of Thee as Thou art expressed in the laws whose manifestations they witness day by day.

Thou art beyond all the teachings of teachers, Thou art beyond the visions of seers, Thou art beyond the restrictions of temples and churches and synagogues, Thou art the Great Spirit Whom we all seek to serve, Whose power we seek to reveal, striving to remind Thy children of their latent divinity within them so that they may find Thee and Thy kingdom.

We strive to teach them to find the power that comes from within, the peace that is within, so that from out of that infinite storehouse they may receive the inspiration to order their lives in Thy service and in the service that Thou would have them render throughout the world of matter.

THOU art the Great Spirit of all life, Who dost reveal Thyself in the simplicity of all things, Whose smile is seen in the faces of children, Whose love is revealed in the love that binds human hearts and makes two as one in Thy sight, in the courage that inspires the children of matter to lay down their physical all to serve Thee and one another.

Oh, Great Spirit, Whose whole universe echoes Thy greatness, the music of nature tries to play Thy symphonies, the sun tries to reveal the beauty of Thy light, and we, who are Thy messengers, try to teach the blind ones the operation of Thy laws.

Great Spirit of all life, give us the power to remove from the eyes of the children of matter the scales which prevent them from seeing Thy beauty and Thy splendour, to make us so strong that we can reveal to them the wonder of Thy love and Thy wisdom, that, putting away the foolish things of matter, they may rise in the fullness of their divine manhood and know that they are a part of Thee, and Thy spirit can shine through them.

OH, Great Spirit, Who dost inspire all those who seek to do Thy will and to lead on the paths of wisdom all those who are serfs in spirit and in body, help us, through Thy power and Thy love and Thy law, to build that temple which will reflect here in this house the light of Thy love, that those whose hearts are sad and whose heads are bowed down with the sorrows of the world, that those whose feet are weary and whose eyes are filled with tears, may come here and find a new understanding and a new purpose and realize that they are a part of Thee, the Great Spirit of all life.

OH, Great White Spirit, Who knowest all things and seest all things, from Whom there are no secrets, Who knowest the unspoken petitions of all Thy children, Who knowest all their wants, Thou has provided, through the operation of Thy natural laws, all that is necessary for their complete sustenance.

Oh, Great Spirit, Who art perfect love and perfect wisdom, Thou dost sustain the whole universe and all that exists in it. Thou hast given to us the task of ministering to Thy children, so that throughout all their earthly lives they may realize that Thy great spirit watches over them, seeking always to lift them up and to point to them the ways of Thy truth.

With their minds filled with the knowledge of Thee and their souls in unison with Thine, and their hearts beating in tune with Thy great heart, may they achieve that unity of purpose, and so be at one with Thy great spirit, that they will know that they are in Thee as Thou art in them.

May the mantle of Thy infinite love cover them, Thy everlasting arms embrace them, and the shelter of Thy knowledge always be above their heads, so that they may know that Thy great spirit is protecting, sustaining and uplifting them.

Oh, Great Spirit, Who, throughout all ages and all times, has poured Thy love through Thy instruments, and has sought to reveal to the children of matter the perfection of Thy plan and Thy design, and has given them freewill, so that they may choose to take part in Thy work, I pray, Oh, Great Spirit, that those who are within the sound of my voice may recognize that here, in this house, they are building a temple, and that hands that do not belong to their world are assisting them to add the stones of truth.

Through the windows of this temple, which are the souls of the children who sit here, the light of Thy infinite truth will be revealed to the children of matter. Oh, Great Spirit, guide their footsteps always. Bring them within the field of Thy infinite love.

OH, Great White Spirit, Thou art the Law behind all life. Thy spirit permeates all the universe. Thou art in everything, whether it registers consciousness in the planes of matter or whether it only registers consciousness on the planes of spirit. Great Spirit, Thou art in all things.

Thou art in the song of birds. Thou art in the rustle of the wind through the trees. Thou art on mountain top. Thou art in ocean depth. Thou art in the ripple of brooks and streams. Thou art in the wind, the air, the lightning and the thunder. Thou art in the sun, in the moon, in the stars and in the sky. Thou art above and Thou art beneath.

Thou art in love, in wisdom and in goodness. Thou art in hate, in envy and in jealousy. Thou art in every human spirit. Thy great spirit fills all Thy universe.

Through the operation of Thy laws we have been enabled to reveal to the children of matter some of the greater glories of the realm of spirit. We have sought to teach them laws through the operation of which they may learn to have a greater understanding of Thee, the Great Spirit of all life.

Throughout all the ages, through all the future yet unborn to the world of matter, Thou art the Great Spirit of all life, the centre of all love, king of kings, more majestic than dreamed by the children of matter. Thy love surpasses their understanding. Thy wisdom crowns the greatest heights they are capable of appreciating. Thy love sustains all things and all life moves because of Thee.

Here in this house we seek to erect a temple filled with Thy power, love and might, that it may radiate into the world of darkness, sending forth streams of light and truth, that those who are in darkness may be illumined by the light of Thy divine truth.

May those whose hearts are sad find, in this place, strength, and those who are weary in spirit or in body find a new strength of spirit; that those who are sad may find comfort and those whose backs are bowed down with care and trouble may learn through Thy laws to seek that new power to guide them.

Oh, Great Spirit of all life, of all love, of all power, of all light and of all goodness, teach us to reveal to the children of earth that Thou art within them, that they may realize how Thou canst shine through them.

OH, Great White Spirit, Thou art the spirit of all life. Thou dost sustain all life because Thou art the natural law of life. Thou art the Lord of life, as Thou art the Lord of death, for in Thy kingdom there is no death except the change which comes from one expression to another.

Thou hast sought to reveal Thyself wherever there have been instruments in the world of matter. Once again, Thou dost seek to pour down Thy love upon all Thy children, so that they may know Thee through the operation of Thy laws, so that they may lift themselves up, so that they may receive more light and more wisdom, so that they may become conscious of Thee within themselves and realize that Thou hast given them a portion of Thyself.

Oh, Great White Spirit, Thou who art the highest of the high and the mightiest of the mighty, Who art the king of all kings, Thou Who art the law that is behind all life, Thou Who art the supreme love, Thou Who art the dazzling radiance of truth, Thou Who art the fulness of all wisdom, we who are Thy servants seek to reveal Thee according to our evolution, so that, because we have grasped more of Thy laws, we can become instruments enabling those who are linked with us in the law of service to work for Thee and for Thy children.

We pray that the power of the spirit which is in our

midst tonight shall enable all those who are within its range to know and to feel that it will uplift them, sustain them, and come like a breath of Thee into their hearts and their souls.

OH, Great White Spirit, Thou art the centre of all life. Thou art the Creator of everything that is, was, or ever will be. Thou hast set all planets in motion. Thy word has caused the stars to be set in their courses, the sun to shine, the wind to blow, the storm to rage, the tides to ebb and flow.

Thou hast given beauty and colour, rhythm and motion to life and endowed it with Thy spirit. Thou art seen in the ever-changing panorama of life as it unfolds itself in all its multitudinous activities.

Thou art the supreme Spirit, the Oversoul, the Infinite Intelligence behind perfect laws in operation. Thou art God and yet so near to each one of us that Thy spirit pulsates in every human being.

Thy consciousness sleeps in a stone; it wakens to its fullest in those beings who, filled with the desire to serve Thee, allow Thy spirit to rise triumphant over all material obstacles and difficulties and express Thee in their lives of self-sacrifice, of altruism, of idealism, of service.

We pay tribute to the perfect laws which mirror Thy

perfection, because we see in them Thy eternal judgment as it doth make itself manifest through life. We know that if all would but allow themselves to live in harmony with those laws Thy will would become manifest.

All the chaos and the misery, the sickness of heart, the weariness of soul, the darkness and the confusion would disappear and the light of Thy truth would shine radiantly in a world of peace, plenty, harmony and love.

And we labour to remove all the limitations that prevent the kingdom of heaven being made manifest on earth; we labour to remove all those vested interests which stand in the way; we labour to replace grief with joy, sadness with happiness, ignorance with knowledge, darkness with light, and bring peace to troubled souls.

We seek to unite all those of goodwill whose desire is to promote well-being; we seek to inspire all who would allow the power of the spirit to move them; we seek to remove the fear of death.

And we seek to build temples not with stone, not with mortar, not with bricks, not with steeples, not with altars, but of willing hearts, aspiring souls, united in love and in the one desire to stimulate the gifts with which Thou hast endowed them, so that they may render service to Thee by serving Thy children.

OH, Great White Spirit, we turn to Thee with prayer on our lips. We do not ask favours of Thee, neither do we present petitions to Thee. Thou knowest the unspoken desires of every soul. No secrets are hidden from Thee.

We desire to lift ourselves up so that we can establish a closer unity with Thy laws and become imbued to the full with Thy power and Thy love.

We strive to present Thee as Thou art, the perfect love behind the perfect law. Thou hast been misunderstood by so many and the eyes of men have failed to glimpse Thee as Thou art. Thou hast been worshipped throughout all ages according to man's understanding, but man has failed to realize Thee as Thou art, the perfect law in operation, changeless throughout all eternity.

Thou art not inaccessible to mankind. Thou art not seated on a white throne far away in the cloudy mists of a nebulous heaven. Thou art not a deified man, with human passions.

Thou art the centre of divinity, which is able to express itself in every being, for Thy spirit is within every child in the great universe.

We strive to awaken that divinity, which has slumbered for too long, that it may recognize its power and so rise to the surface that it will transform and revolutionize every facet of life and bring to an end the constant and recurring discords that make for bitterness, for hatred and for war. For when men have found themselves they have found Thee and that kingdom of heaven which is within them.

We strive to free the spirit from the bondage which men impose on it, that it may escape its thraldom and gain that liberty which is its due, even in a world of matter.

We strive to teach man that within him is a power, a divine power, that can enable him to conquer every difficulty, transform his life and the world in which he dwells, so that it does become an earthly paradise, where there is no strife, no disease, no mourning, and perfect love reigneth among all.

OH, Great White Spirit, Thou art the law, the spiritual law, that rules the mighty universe and all that it contains. Thine is the power that has fashioned the whole system of life; Thine is the wisdom that guides its eternal destiny and Thine is the love that upholds all the systems that it contains.

We who are Thy instruments seek to spread a greater understanding of this Law in all its ramifications, so that Thy children everywhere in the world of matter may adjust their lives and live, not in ignorance, darkness, superstition or fear, but in the knowledge, in the light, in the truth, with understanding in their hearts and in their minds.

We seek to spread the truth which will make men free, so that they may overthrow all those systems which breed selfishness, which cause chaos and disaster, misery and suffering, tears and bloodshed, so that an enduring peace may be their lot.

We seek to comfort those whose hearts are heavy, whose heads are bowed down with grief, whose eyes are filled with tears, so that in the knowledge that love is eternal they may find that solace and consolation that will give them a truer understanding and a rightful perspective of life as it really is.

We seek as always to bring a demonstration of Thy power of the spirit into this world of matter, that men may understand Thou art not far off, removed, inaccessible, but in their midst, within their hearts and souls, in the fibre of their very being, that they may find within their latent divinity strength and courage to uphold them and to enable them to go forth, to battle against all those things which stand in the way of love, wisdom and peace ruling their world.

I PRAY to the Great White Spirit for the influx of His power, for the descent of the Holy Ghost, that we may be enabled to transmit His wisdom, His love and His inspiration, that we may be enabled to reveal Him as the perfect law behind every manifestation of life.

We seek only to serve the Great Spirit by serving His children, so that with knowledge they may drive out the ignorance that prevents them from fulfilling their divine destiny.

We desire to teach them how to find themselves, their real selves, hidden and crushed for centuries behind the barriers of superstition and prejudice and misunderstanding and misconception, so that they may free themselves from their slavery and begin to understand life in all its fullness, its sweetness and its richness.

We seek to bring light into a world that is still full of darkness, that still practises hatred and revenge and has not yet learned how to put into operation in all its fullness the law of love, the only rule by which all Thy peoples can dwell together in amity, concord, harmony and peace.

We seek to destroy all the fear and the terror associated with death, and to reveal death as part of life, so that its purpose may be fully understood by all.

And to Thee, Who art the Great Spirit of all life and hast endowed us with Thy precious divinity and hast fashioned us in the likeness of Thy spirit, we desire to draw closer, so that we can become greater instruments in Thy service, rejecting none and seeking to bring within the radius of Thy law and Thy love and Thy power all Thy children.

We continue our labours, spreading truth wherever we go, until there shall be fulfilled on earth all that was prophesied by those who possessed the vision born of the spirit.

OH, Great White Spirit, we meet here in perfect harmony

in the silence in this sacred place, where the two aspects of life blend and become one, and we seek to find our true selves, knowing that in finding them we shall find Thee, Who art the infinite spirit of all life, reflected in varying degrees in all Thy children throughout the whole universe, throughout the world of matter and the world of spirit.

We return to demonstrate the constancy of Thy laws, so that there may be known for evermore those fundamental spiritual realities upon which life is based.

We seek to bring into operation the power of the spirit, that vitalizing, energizing, lifegiving, vivifying force that can transform all humanity, subdue all the animal instincts and enable the higher divine self to find expression.

We seek to spread the light of truth and to dispel the darkness, so that with knowledge to arm them Thy children may find freedom and liberty. We seek to inspire all those who wage eternal war on the forces of darkness and materialism, of self-interest and greed, of envy, hatred, malice, all those who for too long have held Thy children in their despotic sway.

We work to speed the new world, which spells a new era, a new chapter in human life, that brings a new hope and a new understanding, so that those who are weary in the fight may become refreshed, their tired spirits encouraged and strengthened in the knowledge that Thy plan is nearing fruition.

We desire to reach all those who suffer, who are in sadness and sorrow, the mourner, the hungry, the desolate, the weak, the helpless, those who know not where to turn and who yearn for the light of truth which will enable them to find Thee and themselves.

And we seek always to spread a fuller understanding of Thy eternal natural laws, so that the needless warfare, quarrelling and confusion between the forces of religion may be ended and Thy children learn that in Thy sight there is but one religion—to give service wherever we can.

To that end we pray and labour seeking to draw closer together all those whose objects are the same as ours, no matter who they may be or where they may be.

OH, Great Spirit, Thou art the light of all life. Thy breath is in all life. Thy laws support all life and Thy spirit broodeth over all life.

Oh, Great Spirit, we thank Thee for all the light which has been vouchsafed throughout all the ages of being. We thank Thee for the earthly instruments who have been enabled to register Thy wisdom from on high and to illumine the world of matter.

We thank Thee for all the saints and for all the sages, for all the mediums, for all the inspired ones who have sought to reveal to mankind the fulness of Thy love and of Thy wisdom, who have exhibited in their wondrous lives Thy great spirit. We thank Thee for all the inspiration that has come through all the instruments of all peoples, of all countries and in all languages, knowing that they have all sought to reveal Thee according to their understanding.

Oh, Great White Spirit, we render thanks to Thee because we are able to demonstrate Thy law and Thy love to others, because we are enabled to pierce the world of matter and to lift the veil so that the children of earth can understand more about the eternal things of life, so that they may direct their thoughts upward to the spheres of spirit and fill their minds with Thy wisdom and their hearts with Thy love, so that Thy will shall be done through them.

We thank Thee for Thy power which is vouchsafed to us to enable us to return on wings of love to teach the world of matter the eternal laws of the spirit which will enable them to have peace and happiness and plenty.

We pray to Thee that there shall come all through the world of matter that light from Thee, that love and that peace which will enable all mankind to understand the purpose for which Thou hast placed them on earth, so that they may fulfil Thy will.

May we who seek to serve Thee exhibit all that power, that love, that wisdom, that knowledge which is of Thee, and may we in this temple build a haven where the weary and sad, the distressed and broken, the homeless and the hungry may find that strength which will enable them to raise their heads and know how much they are a part of Thee, the Great Spirit of all life.

OH, Great White Spirit, Thy infinite and wondrous laws sustain us all. Thy love holds us all in its embrace. Thy wisdom guides us. Thy power sustains us. Thy knowledge lights the torch of truth for faltering feet.

We thank Thee for all that we know concerning Thee and Thy manifestations in the realms of spirit and in the smaller world of matter. We thank Thee for the knowledge of Thy perfect law, for that rhythm of perfection which sustains all and contains all, which faultlessly and ceaselessly sustains the whole universe and everything which dwells in it.

Oh, Great White Spirit, we thank Thee for all the revelations of Thyself which Thou hast given us at all times. We thank Thee for the willing servants who have ministered to Thy children of matter and who have sought to uplift them and to draw their eyes to those spiritual truths which alone can teach them how to live their lives in the fulness which Thou hast intended.

Oh, Great White Spirit, who can measure the infinity of Thy wisdom, the perfection of Thy law, the supremacy of Thy knowledge, the eternity of Thy truth? Thou art wiser than the wisdom of all the ages; Thou art more mighty than human minds can comprehend; Thy spirit, which Thou hast placed within all, which enables us to live and to function, eludes the mind of man, which cannot measure it or fathom it.

We thank Thee for the gift of life, which binds us all with one another and which makes us one vast family, which unites us, spirit to spirit, heart to heart, mind to mind, and love to love, across even the gulf of death.

We thank Thee for the chain of human spirits, which is encircled by spirits released from the bodies of matter, of whom Thou art the centre.

Great White Spirit, we pray that each one of us shall draw closer and closer to Thee, feeling the fulness of the benediction of Thy power, knowing that we are linked with Thee for eternity, that we can raise ourselves up to receive more of Thee, more of Thy wisdom, more of Thy power, so that, with our eyes fixed on the spiritual, we can learn eternal truths, and can serve Thee better.

OH, Great White Spirit, the whole of life revolves around Thee, and Thou dost hold in the embrace of Thy love the whole of humanity, whether it expresses itself in the world of matter or in the world of spirit.

Oh, Great White Spirit, Thou art the centre of all life, for Thy being is expressed in all life. Thy spirit giveth life and Thou art life itself, for with Thee there is life, and without Thee, there is nought.

Oh, Great White Spirit, Thy love sustains all things. Thy wisdom has created all things and Thy purpose shapes all things. Thy plan gradually comes into fulfilment as it expresses itself throughout all the spheres of existence.

Thou art the Great Spirit, Who art so great that no mind, however exalted, can understand Thy fulness. Thou art the Great Spirit, and yet Thou art within the smallest of the small as Thou art expressed in the greatest of the great.

Nothing happens in the whole universe that Thou dost not know, for Thy laws embrace all life and Thou, Great Spirit, art everywhere, for Thy spirit pervadeth all things.

And we, who are Thy servants and who seek to express Thy laws, ask of Thee for that power which will enable us to work in co-operation with all willing souls in the world of matter, that we can build stronger bridges between the plane of matter and the plane of spirit, over which many more messengers can return, bringing Thy message of love and goodwill and peace to the world of matter.

Over these bridges may there return not only Thy messengers but also those who belong to those still in the world of matter.

We ask at this time, when all thoughts are centred on the one who came to earth to demonstrate Thy love and Thy power, that the children of earth shall remember that within them is Thy power, which will enable them to sweep away all the obstacles that prevent peace in their world. If they would but reveal Thee in their lives and in their actions, then Thy will would be done.

OH, Great White Spirit, Thy laws uphold all the universe. Thou art responsible for all life, for Thou hast created it. Thou hast endowed the children of matter with Thine own divinity.

Thou hast made them like Thee and placed within their souls the power which unites them with Thee throughout all infinity, so that as they evolve they can become more like Thee.

Oh, Great White Spirit, Thou hast reigned supreme throughout all the ages of time and Thou wilt reign supreme throughout all the ages yet to come, for Thou art the Great Spirit of all life.

Thou dost sustain all things and Thou art manifested in every phase of life, whether it is revealed to the consciousness of those in the world of matter or whether it registers far beyond in the planes of spirit.

Thou hast called us to Thy service so that we, who are Thy messengers, can work to bring Thy will into fruition and can help to reveal Thy plan and make it manifest on earth.

We would co-operate with the children of matter so that they may understand Thee and understand themselves, so that they may replace their systems of hate with love, their selfishness with service, so that they may abolish war and have peace, so that they may abolish starvation and have the plenty which Thou hast showered into the world.

Oh, Great Spirit, we thank Thee for those hours which we spend together with Thy children who dwell in the lower planes of life, for out of their co-operation we shall be enabled to achieve greater things for Thee, to bring succour to the distressed, light to those in darkness, strength to the weak, healing to the sick, peace to those who are in the storms of life.

We thank Thee for this haven of refuge, for this temple of light, and we work to enable all the obstacles that prevent the free communion with the world of spirit to be surmounted, so that Thy will shall reign supreme.

OH, Great White Spirit, we turn to Thee, for Thou art the eternal, unchangeable law. We recognize that none can supplant Thee and Thy creation, for wherever there is life Thy spirit reignest supreme. None can change Thy fixed decree as reflected in the law of cause and effect.

When the minds of men are turned to thoughts of destruction, we would remind them that Thou art eternal creation, that the things which endure are the things of the spirit, that in the end they triumph because they are eternal. Strength and sustenance cometh from Thee, Who art the divine refuge for all.

And so, even in this hour, when darkness has descended on the hearts and minds, indeed, in the lives of many, we strive to reveal those links which bind all mankind with one another and with Thee, that they may remember the common thread of divinity which encompasses the whole of Thy family.

We pray for peace with honour, with justice and with mercy, so that there shall reign in the world of matter the harmony of that fuller life into which so many are being precipitated today.

OH, Great Spirit, Thou has provided us with the means of making Thy power known in all Thy universe. Thou hast, through Thy wondrous love, united those of us who are in the spirit part of Thy kingdom with those who are still encased in matter.

Thou hast revealed to us, through the operation of Thy natural laws, not only how Thou hast made provision for the overcoming of death, but also enabled all those who are released from the world of matter to return and to show that the love of the Great Spirit which emanates from them enables them to rejoin those whom they have left in the world of matter.

Oh, Great Spirit, Thou art enshrined in every human heart, heard in every song of the birds, seen in every manifestation of the wonders of Nature, felt in every note of music and seen wherever the eyes of the spirit are opened.

Oh, Great Spirit, the children of earth have yet failed to understand Thee—they look for Thee in books when they can find Thee in the manifestation of Thy love in the universe; they look for Thee in churches, when they can find Thee in their own hearts; they do not yet realize that Thou art as themselves, spirit as they are spirit, and that they are divine because Thou art divine.

Oh, Great Spirit, Thou hast entrusted all of us with the work of cementing the life in the world of matter with the life in the world of spirit, so that together we can build a temple where Thy light will radiate into the world.

OH, Great White Spirit, how shall the minds of the children of matter comprehend Thy infinity? Where are the words to describe Thy majesty, Thy wisdom, Thy love, Thy truth?

Thou art perfect, and imperfect mind cannot comprehend Thy perfection. Thou art infinite, and finite mind cannot grasp Thy infinity. Thou art divine love, and human love cannot understand divine love.

Thou art the zenith of all wisdom, and the wisdom that is expressed in matter cannot understand the wisdom that belongs to the highest.

But, as great and as mighty and as infinite as Thou

art, Thou art not inaccessible, for Thou art within us all, within every breath and motion and rhythm of life. Thou art within all life in the world of matter, as Thou art within all life in the world of spirit.

Thou art within every nodding flower. Thou art within every rustling tree. Thou art within every whistling wind. Thou art within every twinkling star. Thou art within the roar of the thunder and the flash of the lightning.

Thou art within every rain drop, every song of every bird, within the splash of every stream. Thou art within all, for Thou art the Great Spirit and nothing lives apart from Thee.

Thou art known and realized and understood in the hearts, in the souls and in the minds of Thy children of matter, especially of those who have sacrificed themselves to bring before Thy children Thy love and a knowledge of Thee and Thy wondrous laws that encompass all humanity.

Thou art expressed in the visions of saints, in the dreams of seers, in the music of the inspired ones, in the majestic utterances of poets. Thou art revealed wherever the children of matter reach out in aspiration and desire to attune themselves to Thy divine vibrations.

Through all times Thou hast manifested Thy wisdom to those who could receive it and, once again, the great power of Thy spirit pours itself out on human flesh and men dream dreams and see visions.

The power of Thy spirit reveals the infinite wonder of another life, a life that has been hidden for centuries, a life from which mankind has shrunk with fear and trembling afraid of the unknown.

Great Spirit, Thou hast permitted us, Thy messengers, to return and show that in Thy domain there is no need for fear, for over all, in the world of matter and in the world of spirit, Thy love reigns supreme. Thy love is ever ready to flow and Thy great heart is ready to encompass all, high or low, rich or poor, mighty or small, strong or weak.

Oh, Great Spirit, we rejoice at the many channels through which Thy message is encircling the world of matter, at the new vision that has come, at the new light that is being poured down, at the new truth that reveals itself before the gaze of those who are no longer blind, but can see with the eyes of the spirit the beauties that Thou wouldst have them behold.

And we, who are Thy servants, rejoice that Thou hast permitted us to reveal some of the greater manifestations of Thy kingdom, so that there may be driven from the world of matter all the obstacles that prevent the flow of Thy inspiration and the manifestations of the power of Thy spirit, so that the children of matter may cast off the shackles with which they have bound themselves, so that they may rejoice in the new freedom of their spirit and may realize that they can approach Thee, not only on bended knee but in the knowledge that they are of Thee and Thou, Great Spirit, art of them.

We pray, oh Great Spirit, that in this temple, as in others, there shall come the revelation of Thy spirit which will enable the work which is done here, as elsewhere, to bring comfort to those who are brokenhearted, to bring joy to those whose eyes are filled with tears, to bring strength to those who are weary and a new hope to those who are filled with despair.

Thus shall we help to fulfil the law of service and bring Thy children nearer to Thee, the Great Spirit of all.

OH, Great White Spirit, how shall we explain Thy infinitude to those whose minds are encased in matter? How shall we explain Thee, Who art beyond explanation, Thou Who cannot be measured, Whose wisdom surpasses the wisdom of the highest that is known, Whose love exceeds all that which has been expressed?

How shall we express Thee, the Great White Spirit of all life, Whose spirit pulsates through every manifestation of being, Who art seen in every phase of life, whether it be the life that is known to the world of matter or the life that is revealed in the realm of spirit?

We point to the universe and all that it contains, to the rhythm of life as it expresses itself in every motion. We point to the rising and the setting sun, to the glittering stars in the firmament, to the pattering rain drops, to the ebb and flow of the mighty ocean, to the ripple of the murmuring stream, to the drone of the bee, to the nodding of the flower, to the roar of the thunder and the flash of the lightning.

We point to every manifestation of life and declare that they are expressions of Thee and Thy infinite law, for Thou art law and dost reveal Thyself in immutable, unchangeable, eternal law.

We who belong to the higher manifestations of life return to demonstrate the unbroken sequence of natural law as it is known in the world of spirit. We seek to reveal Thee as Thou art, to demonstrate the superiority of the spirit, to reveal the kinship of the spirit that unites us with Thee, and to make the children of matter realize that they are a part of Thee and Thy spirit broods within them all, ever seeking to find expression.

Oh, Great White Spirit, we pay tribute to Thee for allowing our higher selves to rise to the surface, to seek harmony with Thee, the Oversoul of life. We are reaching out and clasping that which is our divine heritage and finding the reality which is within the depths of every soul.

We pray that in this temple of light we may be enabled to demonstrate some of the laws of the spirit, neglected throughout the centuries but revealed to the few who have sought Thee.

OH, Great White Spirit, we thank Thee for the gift of life. We thank Thee because Thou hast merged Thy spirit into us and enabled us to partake in Thy infinite purpose, helping to manifest Thee, to reveal Thy love, Thy wisdom,

Thy truth and Thy knowledge.

Oh, Great Spirit, we raise our voices in thanksgiving for all the manifold expressions of Thee which are revealed to us in every living phase of the universe. We thank Thee for the opportunity of returning across the gulf of death, over the bridge of love.

We thank Thee for all the willing service that is rendered to Thee and Thy children, whether they dwell in bodies of matter or whether they express themselves in the realm of spirit.

We thank Thee for all those who reveal Thy divinity in their lives and who, because of that, enable their idealism, their nobility and their sacrifice to be an inspiration to others less evolved than they are.

We thank Thee for all the revelations of Thee and Thy infinite purpose given to Thy children throughout every age. We thank Thee for all the acts of martyrdom, of heroism, for all the pioneers and reformers, all who have sought and striven to uplift those amongst whom they dwelt.

We thank Thee for those who have sought to reveal Thy inspiration and to make Mankind understand the laws of the spirit. We thank Thee for all those who, because they lived in the world of matter, have been enabled to confer a boon upon their fellows.

We thank Thee for all the channels between the world of matter and the world of spirit, many unconscious, but all of whom make it possible for a fuller understanding of the great purpose of eternal life to be made manifest.

We thank Thee for the humble and the contrite hearts who seek Thee on devious pathways, sometimes in differing churches and temples, and sometimes professing no religion, but only seeking to express the highest that is within them.

We thank Thee, oh, Great White Spirit, for the opportunity given to us to render service to Thee by serving those whom we love and who aid us to spread knowledge and truth and teach Thy children of matter how to liberate themselves from spiritual bondage and become free.

May all that is done in this temple and other temples speed the day when all mankind, because of their greater knowledge, will dwell in amity, concord and peace and exhibit in their lives that love which comes from Thee, the great infinite love of the Great Eternal Spirit.

OH, Great White Spirit, we praise Thy handiwork in the glittering firmament.

We see Thy beauty in the changing patterns of nature's masterpieces. Thy glory is revealed in the rising and the setting sun, in the stately trees, in the song of birds, in the ebb and flow of the mighty ocean, in the splashing of the little brook.

Thou art in the voice of the storm, in the flash of the lightning. Thou art in every flower and in every droning, winged insect. Thou art in the mighty tempest as Thou art in the gentle dewdrop. Thou art in all beauty and ugliness, in all light and darkness, in all love and hatred, in all ambition and selfishness, Thou art within and without, for Thou dost fill all space and all is Thee, and Thy spirit manifests in every phase of life in the universe.

We pay tribute to Thee because Thou art the infinite Creator and we marvel at the perfection of Thy creation. We seek to reveal Thee as the infinite spirit behind perfect natural law, so that Thy children may realize that Thou art not a god of anger and jealousy and revenge but that Thou art the epitome of perfect love, wisdom and law and, because Thy spirit is behind every manifestation of life, perfect justice rules.

We who strive to reveal the laws that belong to the spiritual realms and their interblending with the world of matter would work to further Thy kingdom on earth, so that in its coming there may be ushered in a new era of peace and harmony and love and co-operation, so that strife, misery, bloodshed, destruction and chaos may disappear for ever.

I PRAY to the Great Spirit, Who has set the whole universe in motion, and Who has placed a spark of His life-giving essence within all of us, that we shall be enabled to attune ourselves to His will, learn His wisdom and bring to all His love, His peace and His blessing, so that our efforts to labour in His service may be crowned with success and many will feel that the load is lightened because of the labours that we perform and our efforts to spread the truths of the spirit into all the corners of the world.

I pray for the descent of the Holy Spirit, that regenerating power that cometh from on high, bringing in its train inspiration, wisdom, comfort, healing, knowledge and truth, so that we shall be enabled to sweep away the limitations imposed on us by the barriers raised by men of ignorance, superstition and of all the forces that belong to the darkness of the night of error.

May the light of divine truth be increased in its intensity because of our joint service, and may the influx of spirit power descend on all those whose hearts and minds and souls are attuned to the vibrations of the higher realm, so that, filled with its energizing power, they will be refreshed and renewed in the great fight that is waged incessantly against all the powers of selfishness, ignorance, vested interest and materialism.

OH, Great White Spirit, Thou art the source of all. Thou art the fountain of all wisdom. Thou art the centre of all knowledge. Thou art the ruler of all life in its many phases. Thou art the divine architect, the supreme ruler, the king of all kings. Thou art master of life and death.

Thou causest the sun to shine, the winds to blow, the rain

to drop from the heavens. Thou dost enable the mighty tide of the ocean to ebb and flow. Thy breath is the rhythm of all life. Thou art revealed in every phase of nature's ever-changing pageant.

We seek to reveal Thee as the Law of all life, so that the children of matter may learn to realize that Thou rulest over all with perfect justice, knowledge, wisdom and serenity, that, because Thou art Law, Thou knowest all, Thou hearest all, Thou seest all and Thou art familiar with the unspoken petitions of every heart.

We seek to reveal Thee as Law so that the children of matter may realize that ultimately divine justice ruleth supreme and that, as long as Thy laws control all phases of life, Thy will shall he done.

May the children of matter learn to live for Thee and for one another and help to bring a greater understanding of Thee into their lives and so help to abolish all the sadness and misery, the distress and the weariness, the chaos and the bloodshed that come because the world of matter will not live according to Thy laws.

We seek to reveal the greater powers of Thy spirit, so that Thy children may understand that they do not grovel in the dust before Thee, that they may know that they are spirit of Thy spirit, that Thou art within them and that they are never separated from Thee, that they are never lost, never out of Thy sight and never beyond the embrace of Thy divine love.

And further, we seek to reveal the operation of those

higher laws, so that once again the world of matter may realize that in Thy domain there is no death but only progressive, unfolding, eternal life.

We seek to bring knowledge where ignorance rules. We seek to bring light where there is darkness. We seek to bring wisdom where there is superstition. And we seek to bring the light of spiritual truth where there is ceremony and ritual only.

TO THE GREAT SPIRIT

Other books which may interest you

Available online from
www.spiritualtruthfoundation.org

Other books which may interest you

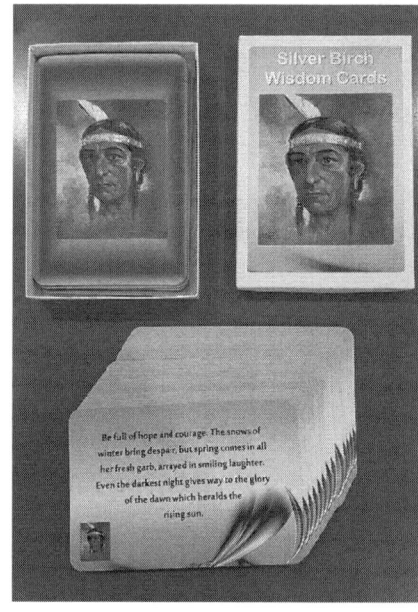

Available online from
www.spiritualtruthfoundation.org

Other books which may interest you

Available online from
www.spiritualtruthfoundation.org